Made in United States
Troutdale, OR
08/24/2023

12339499R00071